Zoe Brooks

Owl Unbound

Indigo Dreams Publishing

First Edition: Owl Unbound
First published in Great Britain in 2020 by:
Indigo Dreams Publishing
24, Forest Houses
Cookworthy Moor
Halwill
Beaworthy
Devon
EX21 5UU

www.indigodreams.co.uk

ISBN 978-1-912876-36-5

British Library Cataloguing in Publication Data. A CIP record for this book can be obtained from the British Library.

Designed and typeset in Palatino Linotype by Indigo Dreams.
Cover design by Ronnie Goodyer at Indigo Dreams

Papers used by Indigo Dreams are recyclable products made from wood grown in sustainable forests following the guidance of the Forest Stewardship Council.

This book is dedicated to the memory of
Elizabeth Webster, the best of teachers.

Everyone is Someone

Acknowledgements

Some poems, or versions of them, have appeared in Grandchildren of Albion (New Departures), People Within (Thornhill Press), The Rialto, Other Poetry, Argo, Aquarius, Joe Soap's Canoe, Pennine Platform, Westwords, The Curlew, Obsessed With Pipework, The Dawntreader, The Fenland Reed, Poetry Birmingham Literary Journal, Prole, Dream Catcher, Northampton Poetry Review, Confluence, Nutshell, South West Review, The New Oxford Magazine, Weyfarers, Understanding, Beach Hut, Words For The Wild, The Lake, and Dear Reader.

Thank you to all my poetry friends, who have supported me in my writing. My special thanks to Christine Whittemore for her feedback about the collection, to Anna Saunders and Angela France for encouraging me to submit my collection to Indigo Dreams, and to Michael Horovitz for giving me the push I needed to start submitting poetry to magazines again. Last but never least my thanks to Philip Wilkinson, for his support, copy editing, mugs of tea, and for just being there.

Also by Zoe Brooks

Fool's Paradise, White Fox Books, 2012

CONTENTS

Naunton Farm 9

My Grandfather and Uncle 10

The Seedsavers 11

Cleeve Hill 12

On Wounded Heads 13

Arthritis and the Flower 14

Junctions 15

Severn Train 16

Fossils on the River Severn 17

Ash Dieback 18

Leaves 19

Betrayal 20

From Streetlamp to Gutter 21

Curriculum Vitae Blues 22

Covent Garden 23

Punch 24

The Baby and the Mushroom 27

Someone Lost 28

The Lost Daughter 29

The Forest 30

The Apples 31

Owl Unbound 32

Too Far 34

Dorothy Wilson Said 35

Meeting on a Summer Evening 36

The Midday Fox 37

The Black Dog 38

Reasons 39

Not Shingles 40

We'll Say No More 41

A Theft 42

Walls 43

Light on the Marriage Bed 44

The Breaking of the Blood 45

Nerve 46

Ultrasound 47

Charlie Watching 48

The Roofer 49

Overloon 50

War Memorial 51

Radio Interview 52

Before Thunder 53

There's Nothing To See 56

Without a Stair 57

The Gypsies in the Room 58

Somerset Beach 59

Owl Unbound

Naunton Farm

Sometimes, still, I come across
your death again.
As I sign executor's deeds,
calculating interest
that is beneath interest,
I discover my mother's words –
"He died today."
And the shock of it
makes my hand pause.
My hand reaches down
to the little cat
with no ears,
which rubs against my ankle crying.
You had hands big enough
to hold that cat
in your palm,
carrying her
away from the burning barn.

My Grandfather and Uncle

My grandfather and uncle
both returned to the earth
with untimely haste.
Although they worked it,
broke its back
for frost to bite into,
dragged sedge from ditches,
clawed back
lambs from snowheaps,
they did not inherit it,
unless it was
in the length and width
of a man's form.
And it claimed them
early,
reaching up through the chest,
pain filling the arms,
which had gathered harvests.
And still they loved it
and still they cursed
on cold wet mornings,
as it worked
like ringworm into their hands.
In death
they shall inherit the earth.
Until this time
they have been living
on borrowed land.

The Seedsavers

In the garden stringed CDs clatter
in the light breeze
flashing low winter sunshine
on to kale leaves.
A horde of starlings loots
the hawthorn bushes.
Inside a circle of women
unmask seeds from pods,
sort, sift, keep and discard.
Their low voices speak
of sons and daughters,
the weather, Christmas and bread.
Their leader worries fine lettuce seed
in a small sieve over a porcelain bowl.
At last she rises
and walks into the garden
sniffing the wind.
Her shed-husband offered
to make a machine once,
but she prefers the ancient way –
the lift of seed, the fall,
the scatter of chaff across the roses.
She turns and returns to the others.
Later, when they depart,
she sees the birds rise
like wheat from the sower's hand,
the rush of their wings overhead
is the sound of grain pouring from a sack.

Cleeve Hill

I found you tiny stars
in the scree of a quarry scrape.
Broken fragments of echinoid stems
sat in my palm
no bigger than breakfast cereal.
Below us an ancient ring ditch
still sheltered the flock,
above us a hawthorn scratched
at clouds with arthritic hands.
The sky roared by
as you said you would make
a necklace of them,
and told me I had fossil eyes.

Years later, after your death,
I found a stone heart
in the shelter of the dip slope
and placed the fossil urchin
above the portal of the tump
where you had lain
on sheep-cropped grass
and said there was no better place.

On Wounded Heads

Coming home between dewfall,
when time became conspicuous
and my forehead flowed in rivers
savagely staining my shirt,
I met a priest walking in the fields.
He carried sea-holly in his hand.
I could see its twisted purple
in a crown of thorns.
He told me, "Kings only rule
that bear their crowns on wounded heads."
Said he was making a hat for St Peter's Day.
I offered him bryony
knowing no other flower.
I offered him elder
though the scent reeled me.
I offered him dock
to calm his wounds.
And three times he denied me.
Over the fields, on the tower head,
the metal cockerel clanged
and shattered the sunlight.

Arthritis and the Flower

In a triangle of wasteland
between platforms,
between the lines of departure,
in the rich green of late summer
Californian poppies flame.
Like the Holy Ghost
they hover above grass heads.
My hands ache at their brevity,
their brilliance and their burning.
Our ways are parted from their ways
by wire fencing and a broken gate.
My hands ache to grasp the flames
and the light dancing within them.

Junctions

You are always here
when I am not.
I am not now
but lost in the railway sidings
between the fox track
and the willow herb.

"She's not with us,"
my mother would say
at the dinner table,
as my fork lay idle
beneath my hand.
"Lost in her own world!"

No world of my creating,
but lost, certainly –
a junction of lines
with the points
frozen.

Severn Train

Gazing from the moving window,
I saw the skull of a sheep
in the brining stream
that slummocked to the river.

I have stood
between those empty eyes,
looking out
at the man
in the knee-deep mud
netting elvers,
while the river
disappeared in mist.
I have longed to leap
into the fast-moving clouds
shadowing the hills.

But, now that you are gone,
I am empty eyes,
empty skull
stuck in mud,
a lamb
who went too far
when the tide was high.

Fossils on the River Severn

The river below us slurps at Jurassic mud.
The devil's podiatrist, it spits out
toenails and ammonites.
A few days ago the high tide
bounded up the cliff face
like an over-eager puppy,
licking the clay until it crumbled
and crashed.

The boy shows me his box of treasures,
curled fossils in bricks of mud.
I tell him that
devil's toenails were oysters.
He is disappointed.
If not the devil
a dinosaur at least,
something as fantastic
as his imagination.
I walk on
under the bladderwrack
large as birds' eggs
festooning the tree branches.

Ash Dieback

Time flickers and reveals
the lines of light about your eyes
and yet no light left within.

It is always so – you and I.
Always the mist shows
the corpses of trees.
Our love is without sap,
like the flayed ash –
without skin
and without leaves,
knuckle-white and brittle.

From afar we watch
the sentinels on the hill,
yet our praying hands
can only imitate the chanting pylons,
cold and bearing fire.

Is it I who brings
this shroud of rain?
I think it must be,
for all I love is grey,
like my ash-stained hands.

Leaves

Overnight the leaves came,
swollen like bodies in the park,
cramming the gutters
and collapsing before transit wheels.

Winter has come suddenly,
though I have counted the colours,
marked their changes.
It is strange
that a defence is needed of autumn,
but here I stand
with winter corpses
whispering at my feet.

And it is strange
that defence is needed
against vainglorious governments
that weigh art with hospital beds
and find both wanting
and less than gold.

Then someone in that ice-bound park
piled the leaves against the fence
and set them alight.
Now the trees are burning
in the dark winter night.

Betrayal

Poems like firecrackers
amaze the crowds:
showers of gold
light the upturned faces.
But in the cold damp mornings
we search the ground.
Gleaners of stars
find singed grass,
a blackened stick or two,
a scent of fire –
nothing more.

We are betrayed
and by our friends' betrayal
we understand
that we do not exist,
turn our faces
to the rainswept streets,
the brack and brimming rivers
and traipse
past the silent mills.

From Streetlamp to Gutter

From streetlamp to gutter
the rain is caught
on lines.
We do not stand
and wait this time.

The boys have dragged their cardboard boxes
under the railway arches and sleep.

We do not hear or see them.

We have homes and trains to go to.
We have rain-soaked coat seams
and hair like wet satin.
We are not warm,
yet warm enough to make us
not stand a moment longer,
not stand and wait at all.

Curriculum Vitae Blues

Curt morning
day's disease.
Let us painfully assume
certainties.
Like all those joggers
grasping crisp morning air
in clenched and sticky fists,
running as if
they were going somewhere.
Let us bury
our hopes
in gasping breaths
trying to beat ourselves.

Covent Garden

How souls may derive
        life from stones
        none will say.
And yet they do.

Tradition haunts the market still
        and stands in wine bars
        like a lost drunk soul
        searching for bit work
        hauling crates of apples
        and cabbages.
The drinkers do not see him there
        nor the fat woman
        with hair of matted reeds
        dancing at the amplifier's right hand.
The buskers are managed now
        and the pigeon-shat stones
        cleaned down.

But the ironmonger still plunges
        his bleeding finger into patent glue.
"Souls may give life to stones yet,"
        I cry.
"Pootcha, pootcha, pootcha,"
        says old man Punch.
"That's the way to do it."

Punch

1
In the beginning
when God rested from his labours
Adam took a knife and cut down a young elm.
This was his first act of destruction
and Adam smiled at the sap in it
and saw that it was good.
Adam took again the knife
and carved in his own image
a wife beater and a layabout,
a preserver of sausages
and a counter of bodies.
Then as Adam sat outside
the closed gates of Eden
just for the hell of it
he gave his creation
a stick to beat the Devil with.

2
Punch sat at the window
watching the street below.
In the hot September night
he heard windows breaking
and the crash of stones
on riot shields.
A bottle landed beside him,
empty,
a waste if ever he saw one.
He decided to join the fun
and took up his long stick.
"If you can't join 'em,
beat 'em,"
said Punch.

3

Punch was fed up.
He had damp rot
in both legs
and woodworm in his nose,
worse still
him downstairs
had very cold hands.
He switched on the television,
which had fallen
from a broken shop window.
"Theatre is dead,"
said Punch.
"I will enter the movies!
Death Wish V and Blood Lust III –
that's the life for me."
"You're too old,"
said Judy.
"Then I'll enter politics,"
said Punch.

4

Punch stood on a ladder
trying to paint the town red.
Above him the policeman and the bailiff,
the hangman and the Devil
stood on his fingers and ground them flat.
Punch wanted to take his long stick
and knock them down.
But that was just a show,
something to feed the stupid crowds.
It was different here.
So he stood on Judy's fingers instead
and beat the baby,
and he said,

"That's the way to do it."
The policeman and the bailiff watched amused.
They'd get the bastard some time,
no need now.

5
Punch screamed abuse
and the people laughed at him.
The louder he shouted
the more they laughed.
After the show
he sat on a bench
in the dim light of the booth.
Beside him in a glass of gin
sat his voice, slightly stained,
a piece of bent tin bound
like a wound by a reed of cloth.
Punch took up his big stick
and smashed the glass.
He wanted to bellow like a bull,
but his own voice lay there
laughing.

The Baby and the Mushroom

Inside the womb
like a closed room
locked from the outside,
an inner web of fine mesh
enclosing and guarding its secret,
the child waits,
crouched, ready to leap
like a bird into the sky.
Muscles tensed,
mind not yet unfolded, but formed,
to be moulded by time and place
and words, like a potter's fingers.
Fate formed too
a thin line to be kept to.
Baby fingers now search for an opening
in the web.
It leaps into a sky grey with atoms.
New breath halts,
chokes in a big mushroom.
The potter's fingers dig too deep.
Little skull breaks.
The pot cracks.
Clay splatters into atom particles.
On and on, bottomless pit;
man's fingers, man's pots,
are shaped like mushrooms
or babies.

Someone Lost

All round the statue
pigeons hammer at air.
Purgatory is a place of silence,
a place of statues.
They move their bodies into the sun,
not looking up, but
feeling the warmth, knowing it is there.
The jagged brokenness of the paper
that litters the step swirls as
the child looks up,
first to the sun
then to the statue
and question marks it why.
She runs to the hand
warm, laughing at the pigeons.
Why?
We always remember,
but the death of a child
spoils its meaning
and we lock up the doors.
We will bear the scars on our hands,
where the child reached
and held.

The Lost Daughter

The female body is 55% water. The rest is dust.

The fullness in the throat will not be cleared.
Deep in the night,
when the farm dogs clamour at the moon,
the throat tightens and contracts.
Under the floorboards
the dark heaves and swells.
This fullness, this emptiness.
You clear your throat,
and still the dark swells.
You have dust in your throat.
Whose dust?
Whose dust rises in moonlight?
Whose dust lies upon lungs,
clogs veins, fills your head with fears?
There are so many images
that in the night sidle between the sheets.
In the day perhaps they can be put aside,
wiped from the window like condensation.
You rise and rinse her out of your throat.
But then the dust gathers again
and the panes mist over.
The drops join and begin to flow.

The Forest

Caught in the spiral of notes, she
screamed.
Captured in the lock of time, she
was agitated.
So in the density, she
sought herself.
In the perplexity of leaves,
hanging like men, she
clung to her faith.
One by one the leaves fell, she
was alone again.
The dew rose, she
survived.

The leaves relaxed on the branches, she
was accustomed.
They hung like veils over widows' faces, she
listened to their words.
The seasons rose like four suns, and she
was contented.

The Apples

The apples lie coffined in their boxes
at the head of the stairs.
Sometimes she comes and turns them over,
throwing away the bad.
The white foam of fungus however
still hangs in the air
and infects even my clothes with its sticky scent.

Come Christmas a few will still be there,
like rows of shrunken heads;
their leathery and wrinkled skins,
having resisted my mother's prodding inspection,
will be peeled off in helterskelter skeins
to make mince pies and lovers' names.

A child, I loved the smell of their sweet decay,
as Schiller did, waiting
for words to come to him.

Owl Unbound

First we found the snake
a ball of coiled skin and muscle
in a pickling jar at the base of the hedge.

I followed my father up
the outside stair to the stable loft,
on one side the railway signal
without a track,
on the other a brick wall,
pocked as the moon,
that would crumble
like cheese in the rain
under the thud of my ball
and send it flying sideways
escaping me.

The tread creaked as my father entered
and I followed into the dim.
I looked around, but saw
only an empty perching post.
The owl had gone with its master.

At my father's instruction
I held out my hands
as if ready to receive bread and wine,
but into my bowl of fingers
he dropped a pellet,
a galaxy of small bones and feathers
cocooned in fur.

That night I woke.
The moon shredded by clouds
hung over the stable roof
and an owl called unbound
from the cypress tree.

Too Far

All summer I hunted
the brown pebble-flecked trout
in the headlong rushing stream.
The boy with his rod and barbarous hook
mocked my seaside net.
But he gave up within a week,
while I continued to dip
for the dappled flash of fish.
Deceived by water refraction,
I pursued them,
always too late, too near, too far.
Until one day,
with early autumn and the threat of school
hanging in the brambles,
I slowly drew my net
under the overhanging roots.
The fish nearly pulled
the green plastic mesh
from the bamboo pole,
as I heaved it out of the water.

What was I to do with it?
As I looked at the sequinned trout
drowning in air,
I was ashamed.
I lowered the net into the stream
and let my childhood slip
into the shadows.

Dorothy Wilson Said

Dorothy Wilson said
if you swung hard enough
you would go in a circle
right over the apple branch.
But I knew she was lying.
I knew the jolt at the top,
that suspense before falling back,
the disappointment.

After Dorothy Wilson left for Wales,
I swung so hard
I flew over the Black Mountains
to the sea.

Meeting on a Summer Evening

Between garden and suburban skip
upon the grey-lichened fence
a stag beetle in elegant pose,
chestnut brown
in his Black Prince armour.
Shocked by the size of him,
we stopped to watch
as the antlered knight
in predatory stance
swept the air about his head,
as soldiers cut sandbags
to remove the guts of enemies
hidden there.

Meanwhile slowly
beneath our notice
blacker and larger
than her mate
another climbed the nearby tree.

The Midday Fox

My demon is in the garden.
Nonchalant in the noon-day sun
he bites burs from his fur
and snaps at fleas.
Not quite a fox
he grins at me in the window.
All the time by the fence
the cat watches, waits,
pretends not to care.
My demon came out of the brambles
by the skeleton of the bomb shelter;
under the ash trees
he waits for me.
The autumn sun slopes
over the roof tops;
the light collects in pools.
Over the compost heap
through the flies
my demon goes,
without a backwards look.

The Black Dog

My sister saw him first:
the black dog at the window,
red eyes and mouth the line
where lava meets the sea,
steam on the glass.

He hunts for wolves
that walk on hind legs
through shopping arcades,
buying phone covers,
trinkets, memory cards.
The thud of his tail rattles A-boards.
The retch of his breath
invades the perfume counter.

He merges into darkness,
disappears for years,
months, minutes,
but he is still there
just beyond sight.
He comes to a whistle
we do not hear,
do not know we are making.
When I kiss, I must remember
to breathe in, not out,
for fear I call him.

Reasons

Shall I give you reasons?
There are none.
I do not swerve
to avoid potholes.
I do not swerve
to avoid ramps.
I swerve
to avoid a paper bag lying
like a broken man
in the middle of the road.
I swerve
to avoid you.

Not Shingles

One moonless night
I thought or believed
your love had burrowed
into my nerves
like shingles,
stinging and burning,
when all it was
was a midge bite
where the waistband
revealed flesh
slick with sweat.

We'll Say No More

Let us understand each other
well enough.
There is an understanding
that exceeds the bounds.

When in forgetfulness
my tongue outstrips
my heart
put your lips against my lips
and we'll say no more.

In New Mexico
line upon line
of refined steel poles
search the air
for sudden southern lightning,
and thus we are
searching in each other's mouths
for words
that will crash upon us
anyhow.

A Theft

I stole the moon last night,
shoved it up my sleeve
and slipped away home.
It swims in the bowl
like a fat goldfish
quietly circling.
The news anchor announces
its disappearance.
The screen shifts to beaches
unwashed,
to surfers bereft.
But in my room
the water rises and falls
lapping at the glass rim
and I feel the tide of blood
rush in my veins.

You look up at the screen
and then away again.
You do not see
the light flooding the room
nor the moths battering
the window.

I stole the moon for you,
but you did not even notice.

Walls

Through the walls
my neighbours
make love.
Her cries
cling
like the trail of snails
upon the kitchen floor,
clear, transparent,
hard to brush off,
as I lie
empty in the night.

Light on the Marriage Bed

Light askant
through ash leaves
like water shine
on my empty sheets.
I lean to smooth
the cotton down.
I am smoothing the sea
and I smell you in it,
as I would smell salt
and the flood.

The Breaking of the Blood

It is very clear to me,
as it is clear to all of us –
that memory
of the first trace of blood.
It was a surprise,
as it is always a surprise
for each woman
that comes upon herself
with the breaking of the blood.
And I thought, as I gazed
at my blood upon the water,
of the time
when reaching
into fine white snow
my hand found glass.
I thought
of a child's fairytale –
of a queen at a window
wishing herself a child –
snow-white
and lips of blood.

Nerve

Nerve trapped
deep at the foot
of my spine,
as bones part
easy, easy,
to allow
the slip and pull,
the tear of child,
living still,
growing already,
placing the press
of self
on my body.

I hardly know you
but my nerve trapped,
the slip of my bones
to allow your head,
impress your will
on mine.

Ultrasound

Refracted by water
like a silver fish,
not pausing beneath sounds,
turning which way.
Through darkness,
through warm waters,
and the constant beat of my heart,
you flash fast.

"We've a wriggler here,"
she says,
seeking you out
like a shoal of cod.

Then suddenly you are still
and stand clear
upon the screen
– a small child
with head and flickering heart.

We measure the circumference
of your skull,
your femur and spine.

It is not time yet
to draw you in,
into this cold air-bound world.

Charlie Watching

Rummy shuffles forward.
In the gaslight all things are black and white,
all things flicker,
all things are blurred at the edges.
Rummy by name and rummy by breath,
his tread is unsteady.
He has feet the size of marrows
in black broken boots.
A small man, he has a giant's trousers.

The gentleman of the halls
calls Rummy over.
The man's tie pin is made of silver,
his woman of full flesh
and fuller pleasure.
The gentleman offers a penny
with a bejewelled hand.

In the gaslight all things disappear –
the gentleman's chequered suit,
the horse's sweat,
the woman's stark perfume.
In the gaslight all things fade but this –
Rummy's splayed feet,
the dark coal smudges of his eyes
and baggy trousers.
All things are forgotten,
but Rummy
and the little boy in the shadows watching.
Charlie watching.

*When I saw Rummy shuffle his way across the pavement to hold a cabman's
horse for a penny tip, I was fascinated* ~ Charlie Chaplin

The Roofer

He rides the roof side-saddle,
one leg hoist beneath him,
the other outstretched
tiptoeing the thin laths.
Above him the clouds buck
and gallop,
the wind careening the trees.
He is nonchalance and ease.

He could swing his leg over the ridge
and grasping the pommel
reach up to wipe the clouds
(they are fleeing already)
from the sun's face
and pocket it.

But he is a man not of light but stone,
prising off the tiles
with rook-beak hammer.
He weighs them in his hand
discarding the bad
keeping the good.
"These," he says to his mate,
"will last another hundred years."

Overloon

In her redbrick bungalow
a half-crazy old woman
saw her madonna cry.
And now they come –
the freaks and the cripples.
I have heard
the long unending cry
of the stones of Overloon.
Along the road the pilgrims come –
the Totenkopf and Ursulines.

I would like to write
a poem against the sword,
but if I did,
children would climb upon it
and pretend to be soldiers;
I would hear the rattle of skulls
beneath their crowding cries.
Along the road the pilgrims come –
the Totenkopf and Ursulines.

Anyone could say my poem
in a monotone,
carefully observing the rhythm,
throwing away lines
with theatrical slickness;
but I want someone,
who can speak with the cadences
of a lung entered,
of a bayonet-gushing throat.
Along the road the pilgrims come –
the Totenkopf and Ursulines.

Overloon was the site of a vicious World War II battle involving the Waffen SS (the Totenkopf).

War Memorial

Above the memorial
"To those who gave..."
a dead sparrow
is huddled
like a small
clenched fist.

Radio Interview

Not quite my father's voice,
its depths broken
by a charge of illness.
I hear it now,
as I failed to hear then
or chose not to,
the muffler of morphine,
as if the tongue was larger
than the mouth
and cannot strike
the waiting teeth.
He retells memories,
tales eternal in their repeating,
the burr of childhood
sticking to the radio speakers.
Still I smile at it,
remembering being held,
a bear cub on his chest,
feeling the reverberation
of his voice against my cheek.

Before Thunder

In dank waters
hands float like lilies.
And the Tigris,
that bore civilization
like mother earth
on uneven shoulders,
runs, a brown wound,
between factions.

Wasps swarm
above my lover's window.
They have made their home
above our bed.
Next year they will swarm
in some other place.
Above your grave, I wonder.

Such fertility in me –
my mind bleeds words.
In the bushes beyond gardens
a vixen screams in the dark,
engendering, and endangering night.

There's no answer to it.
I want wit less than justice
and wit enough to bear it,
a sudden lightning flash
breaking into the music
like a stutter.

The sky is dark tonight.
The sky is full of dust
and thunderflies.

The light is reflected
like a giant moon
curved as a woman's belly.
Man is always deceived
by mirrors that pretend
to be windows.

My keys lie next
to glass and comb.
I could take them up
and drive down
the night-time fox
and moths like ticker tape.
I could drive myself down,
draw the sheets of lightning
over my head
and close my eyes.

Women bear their destruction
within them like rotten fruit.
There is a sweetness there
that exceeds taste.
Only the snake can get
his tongue about our seed.
And there is a bitterness
that exceeds gall.
The wasp eats all
and then moves on.

It has become hard for me
to speak of it.
Your blood beat overtakes mine
and then suddenly I wait,
as an audience at the final note,
as children delighted and scared
before thunder.

We demand continuity
and we are denied
by blood and by music.
We fill finality
with stupid applause.

There's Nothing To See

I have taken off my body
and hung it on the wardrobe door.
It has become too much for me.
I am tired of pulling it on
each morning rumpled by sleep.

I have worn it so long
it has lost its shape.
Threads have caught and drawn,
patches rubbed bare,
each fold a place for shadows to hide.

I pass the mirror in the hallway
and there's nothing to see,
nothing to catch on the parquet floor
nothing to mark the doormat
as I walk outside.

Without a Stair

The grandchildren see her failing light
flickering on a landing without a stair.
We, the daughters, put up ladders,
climb to bring food, hammers and wet wipes.
We sit in the antechamber
watching her hands flick and dance
across the blanket, her lips moving,
song words remembered,
music a bridge across the gaping floor.
We hum along to Jim Reeves,
remembering her warm kitchen,
Mum dancing over the lino,
cheese on toast for tea,
and Family Favourites on the BBC.
She made our home an ark,
built it strong with seasoned wood.
She is still there
in her house on a crumbling cliff.
Some time soon it will float out to sea.

The Gypsies in the Room

It is the unstitching
of the mind,
we tell ourselves, watching
as she slips further from us,
like an old purse,
the lining opening
to reveal lost coins.
Morphine and dementia
see the Gypsies in the room,
silent in a row.
The ancestors come to greet her,
we joke,
to watch over the journey
we cannot take with her,
not yet anyway.
The coins jingle,
crossing the palm
of the ferryman.

Somerset Beach

A mist curls where
sandstone cliffs
born of deserts
meet the cold wash
of the Atlantic.
The tide reveals
plates of grey lias,
stacked stone books
slipping into pools,
where oystercatchers pick
at the slate sheets,
searching for winkles
among ammonites.
Time slips here too.
It coils like the fossils,
a fractal spiral
endless and returning.

Take the path from the beach,
past the shale kiln with ivy
smoking from the chimney,
past the teashop couched
in a chantry's broken walls.
Do not pause.
You will be lost here,
a grain of sand in a galaxy.

Indigo Dreams Publishing Ltd
24, Forest Houses
Cookworthy Moor
Halwill
Beaworthy
Devon
EX21 5UU
www.indigodreams.co.uk